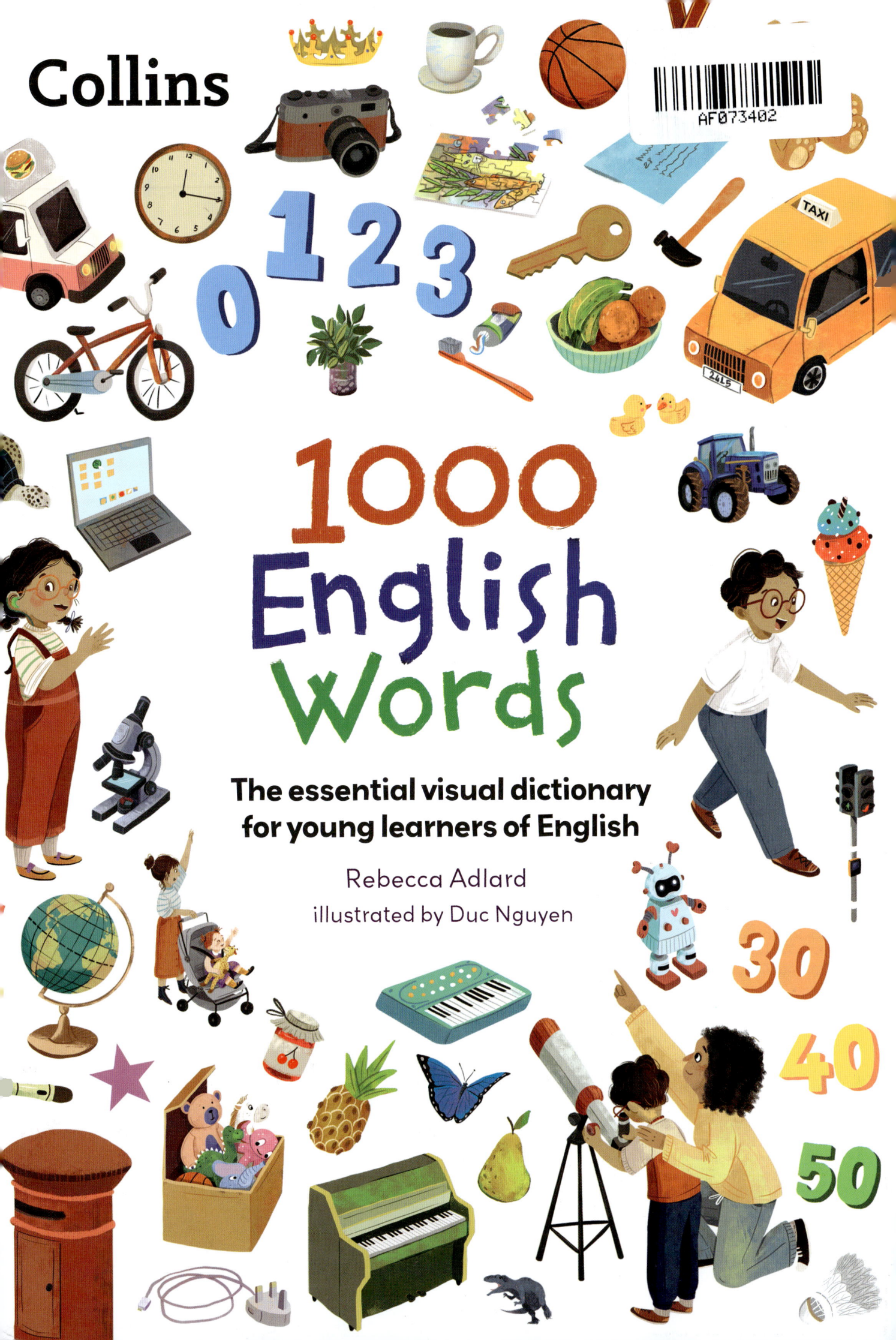

1000 English Words

The essential visual dictionary for young learners of English

Rebecca Adlard

illustrated by Duc Nguyen

Collins

Published by Collins
An imprint of HarperCollins Publishers
1 Robroyston Gate,
Glasgow
G33 1JN

HarperCollins Publishers
Macken House
39/40 Mayor Street Upper
Dublin 1
D01 C9W8
Ireland

First Edition 2026

10 9 8 7 6 5 4 3 2 1

© HarperCollins Publishers 2026

ISBN 978-0-00-875633-8

Collins® is a registered trademark of HarperCollins Publishers Limited

collins.co.uk/elt

Typeset by QBS Learning

Printed in India

All rights reserved. No part of this book may be reproduced, stored in a retrieval system, or transmitted in any form or by any means, electronic, mechanical, photocopying, recording or otherwise, without the prior permission in writing of the publisher. This book is sold subject to the conditions that it shall not, by way of trade or otherwise, be lent, re-sold, hired out or otherwise circulated without the publisher's prior consent in any form of binding or cover other than that in which it is published and without a similar condition including this condition being imposed on the subsequent purchaser.

Without limiting the exclusive rights of any author, contributor or the publisher of this publication, any unauthorised use of this publication to train generative artificial intelligence (AI) technologies is expressly prohibited. HarperCollins also exercise their rights under Article 4(3) of the Digital Single Market Directive 2019/790 and expressly reserve this publication from the text and data mining exception.

Entered words that we have reason to believe constitute trademarks have been designated as such. However, neither the presence nor absence of such designation should be regarded as affecting the legal status of any trademark.

The contents of this publication are believed correct at the time of printing. Nevertheless, the publisher can accept no responsibility for errors or omissions, changes in the detail given or for any expense or loss thereby caused.

HarperCollins does not warrant that any website mentioned in this title will be provided uninterrupted, that any website will be error-free, that defects will be corrected, or that the website or the server that makes it available are free of viruses or bugs. For full terms and conditions please refer to the site terms provided on the website.

A catalogue record for this book is available from the British Library.

If you would like to comment on any aspect of this book, please contact us at the given address or online.
E-mail: collins.elt@harpercollins.co.uk

Acknowledgements
We would like to thank those authors and publishers who kindly gave permission for copyright material to be used in the Collins Corpus. We would also like to thank Times Newspapers Ltd for providing valuable data.

AUTHOR
Rebecca Adlard

ILLUSTRATORS
Duc Nguyen (Beehive Illustration)
Lee Teng (Beehive Illustration)

DESIGNERS
James Hunter
Kevin Robbins

CONTRIBUTOR
Maree Airlie

FOR THE PUBLISHER
Gillian Bowman
Kerry Ferguson
Fiona McGlade

Contents

How to use this book   4

Let's get started
My family   8
Days of the week   10
Months of the year   11
Weather   12
Times of day   12
Time   13
Seasons   13
Prepositions of place   14
Directions   15
Numbers   16
School subjects   18
Shapes   19
Parts of the body   19

Our home
Where we live   20
In the bedroom   22
In the bathroom   24
In the living room   26
In the kitchen   28
In the home office   30
The garden at night   32

At school
In the classroom   34
An art lesson   36
In the cafeteria   38
Sports day   40
Time to dress up   42
A school show   44
A game of football   46

Places we go
At the park   48
At the beach   50
At the sports centre   52
At the health centre   54
At a restaurant   56
At the funfair   58
At a party   60
On a picnic   62

Out and about
At the train station   64
In the city centre   66
On the road   68
At the shopping centre   70
Around the town   72
At the market   74
On the farm   76

The world around us
In the desert   78
In the mountains   80
In the countryside   82
Under the ocean   84
In the grasslands   86
In the rainforest   88

Index   90

How to use this book

Hello!

Welcome to your **Collins 1000 English Words** visual dictionary!

In this book, you can see Oscar and Mia in lots of different places. They see, do and learn lots of things. Come with them!

Listen to all the words at **collins.co.uk/eltresources**

Read the title.

At the park

Track 28

path

puddle

48

There are lots of pictures in this book. They will help you to learn English.

Look at this picture from the book. Can you find Oscar and Mia?

How to use the index

If you want to find what page a word is on, use the index. The index is on pages 90–96.

Think of the first letter in the word you are looking for. Find the letter in the index.

Think of the second letter of the word you are looking for. Find words with these two letters in the index.

line n	46–47
lion n	86–87
[to] listen v	44–45
little adj	60–61

Find the word you want.

What type of word is it? Look at page 7 to find out about types of words.

light adj	32–33
light n	44–45
line n	46–47

Some words can be both a noun and an adjective or a verb.

basketball n	52–53
bat (animal) n	32–33
bat (sport) n	52–53
bath n	24–25

Some nouns can mean two different things. When you see a noun two times, look for the word or words that tell you what each meaning is.

line n	46–47
lion n	86–87
[to] listen v	44–45
little adj	60–61

Where can you find the word in the book? Look at the page numbers.

 You can see all of the words from the index at **collins1000englishwords.com**. To find out more about a word, you can click on it to see it in a dictionary.

Types of words

This book has different types of words.

There are NOUNS.

We use noun words to talk about a person or a thing, for example: Mia or tree.

This is **Mia**.   This is a **tree**.

There are ADJECTIVES.

We use adjective words to tell us more about a person or a thing, for example: big or small.

The tree is **big**.   Mia is **small**.

There are VERBS.

We use verb words to say what a person or thing does, for example: brush or ride. In this book, the verbs have the word 'to' before them, for example: to brush.

Mia **brushes** her hair in the morning.   Oscar and Grandad **are riding** their bikes.

There are also pronouns (for example, *me*), numbers (for example, *ten*), prepositions (for example, *on*) and phrases (for example, *half past*).

Look in the index if you want to find other types of words in the book.

Type of word	In the index
adjective	*adj*
adverb	*adv*
noun	*n*
number	*num*
phrase	*phr*
plural noun	*pl n*
preposition	*prep*
pronoun	*pron*
verb	*v*

My family

Track 01

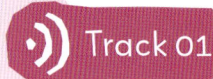

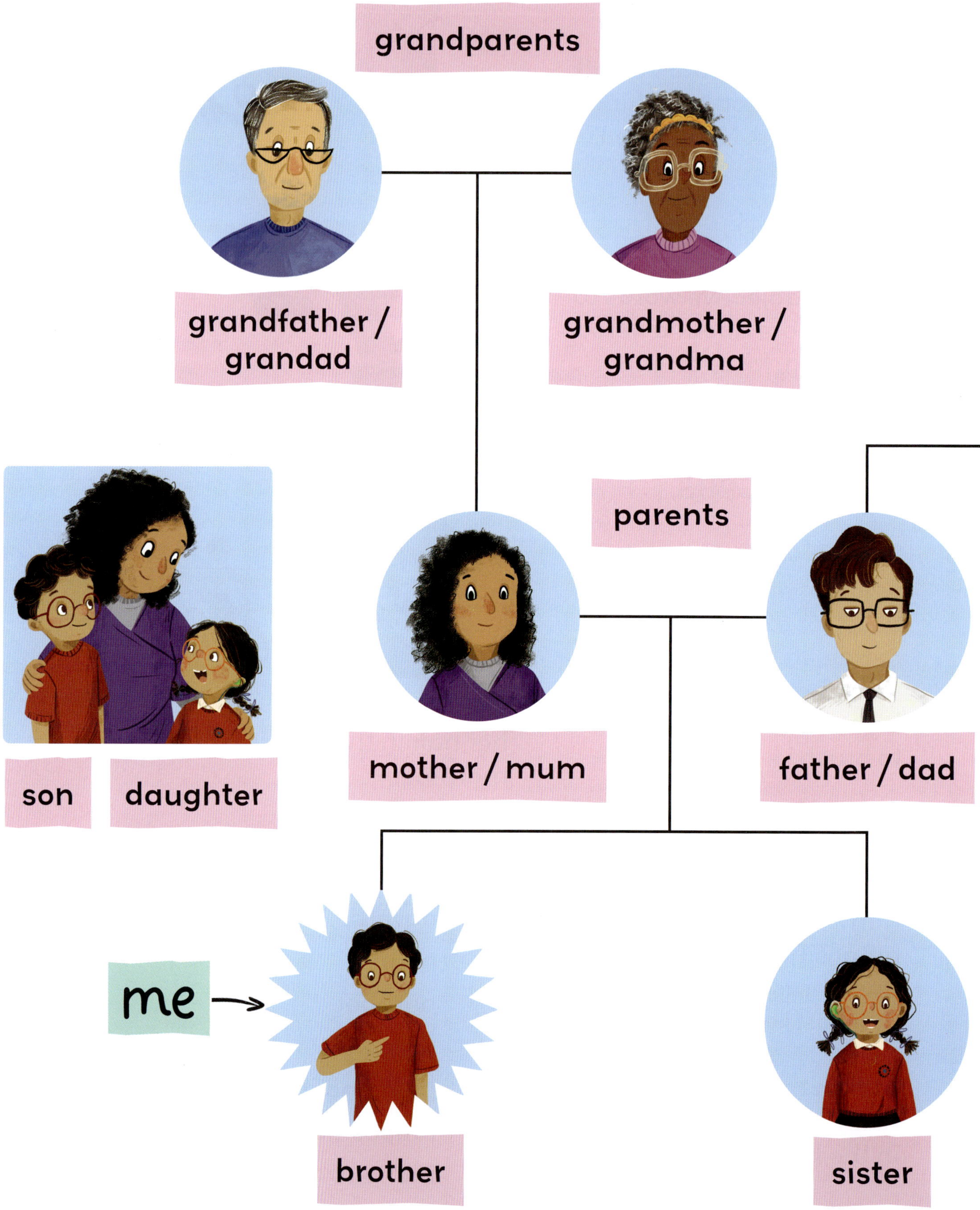
grandparents
grandfather / grandad
grandmother / grandma
parents
son
daughter
mother / mum
father / dad
me
brother
sister

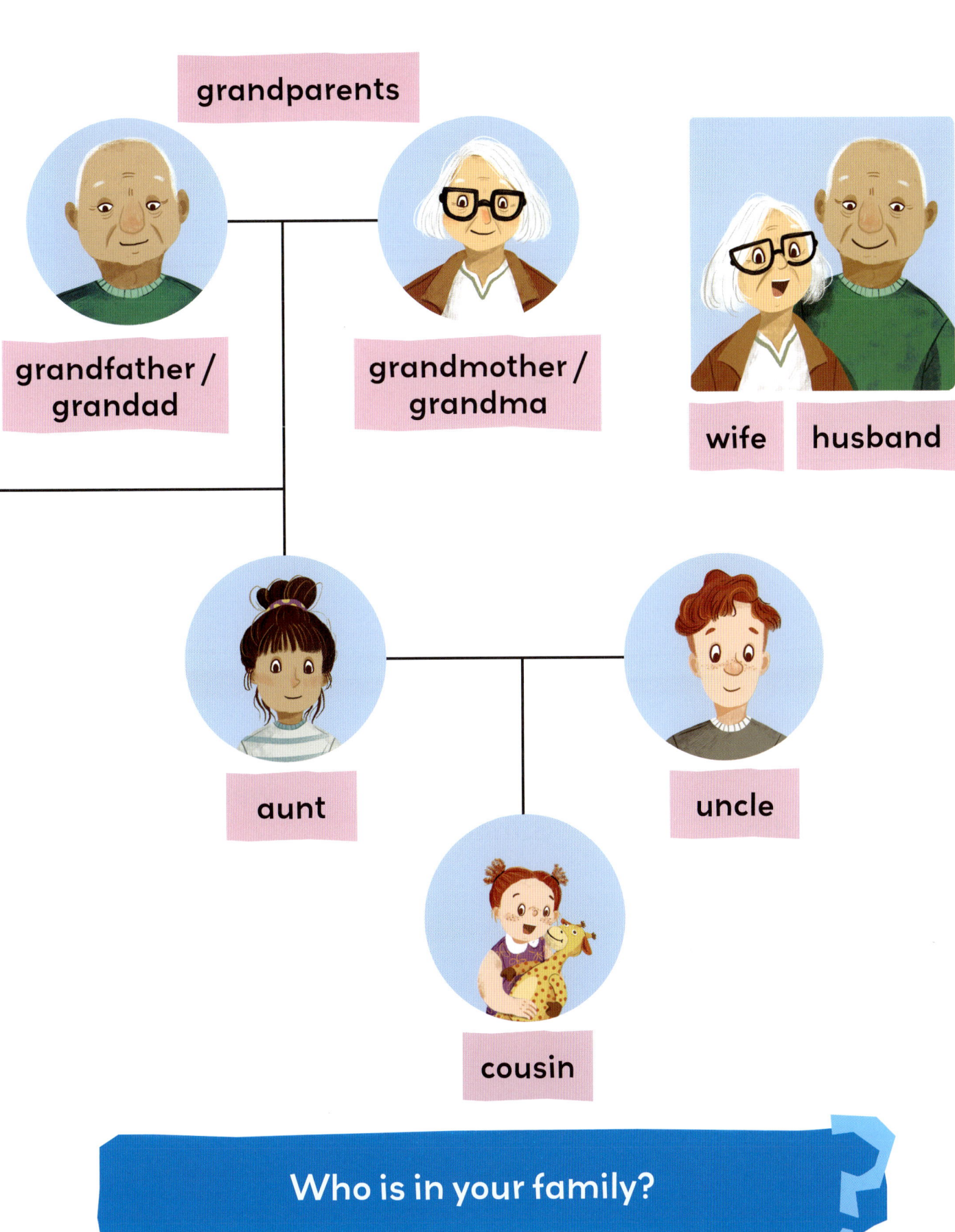

Days of the week  Track 02

[Planner image showing: Monday 10, Tuesday 11, Wednesday 12, Thursday 13, Friday 14, Saturday 15, Sunday 16]

Monday

Tuesday

Wednesday

Thursday

Friday

Saturday

Sunday

weekend

What days are the weekend in your country?

Months of the year

- January
- February
- March
- April
- May
- June
- July
- August
- September
- October
- November
- December

calendar

What is your favourite month?

Let's get started

Weather

 sunny
 raining
 windy
 snowing
 cloudy

 icy
 stormy
 foggy
 hot
 cold

Times of day

 day
 night
 morning
 afternoon
 evening

Time

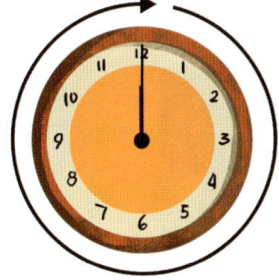

| minute | hour | midday | midnight |

| o'clock | quarter past | half past | quarter to |

Seasons

| spring | summer | autumn | winter |

What are the seasons like in your country?

Let's get started

Prepositions of place  Track 08

behind

between

in

in front of

on

under

above

below

opposite

Numbers

 zero

 one

 two

 three

 four

 five

 six

 seven

 eight

 nine

 ten

How old are you?

11 eleven   **12** twelve   **13** thirteen

14 fourteen **15** fifteen   **16** sixteen

17 seventeen **18** eighteen   **19** nineteen

20 twenty   **30** thirty   **40** forty

50 fifty   **60** sixty   **70** seventy

80 eighty   **90** ninety   **100** a hundred

What number can you count to in English?

Let's get started

School subjects  Track 11

art

computing

PE (Physical Education)

maths

English

geography

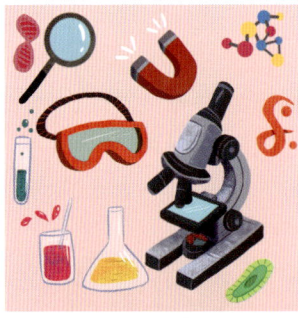
science

history

Which school subjects do you like?

Shapes

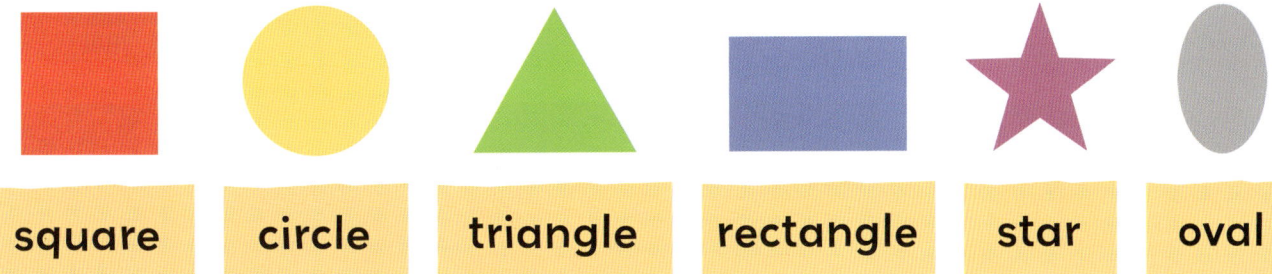

square   circle   triangle   rectangle   star   oval

Parts of the body

ear
face
neck
shoulder
arm
hand
knee
ankle

nose
teeth
hair
elbow
back
leg
toe

head
eye
mouth
finger
stomach
foot

Let's get started

Where we live

Track 14

 car
 key
 delivery driver
 letter
 door
 letter box
 doorbell
 neighbour
 doormat
 postal worker
 fence
 postbox
 gate
 streetlight
 house
 window

How is where you live the same as where Oscar and Mia live?

Our home

	chest of drawers		robot
	doll		shirt
	dress		slipper
	dressing gown	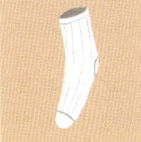	sock
	to get dressed	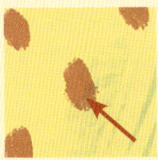	spot
	to get up		teddy
	hairbrush		toy box
	jeans		toys
	keyboard		trousers
	pillow		T-shirt

What have you got in your bedroom?

Our home

	bathmat		soap
	to brush		tap
	comb		toilet
	cupboard		toilet paper
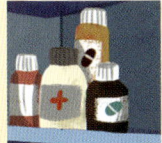	medicine		toothbrush
	mirror		toothpaste
	scales	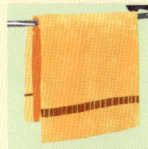	towel
	shampoo		to wash
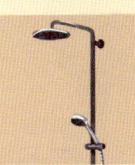	shower		water
	wet		dry

What have you got in your bathroom?

Our home

In the living room

Track 17

bookcase

hall

sofa

board game

26

film

carpet

 armchair    photo

 book    picture

 clock    plant

 comic    popcorn

 cushion    remote control

 dinosaur    stairs

 flower    table

 lamp    television

 magazine    vase

 mobile phone    to watch

What is your favourite film to watch at home?

Our home

dishwasher

	bowl		honey
	bread		jam
	cereal		kettle
	coffee		microwave
	cooker		milk
	cup		pot
	egg		radio
	frying pan		sugar
	glass		tea
	homework		toast

What do you eat for breakfast?

Our home 29

video game

games console

 battery
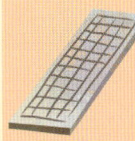 keyboard
 to charge
 laptop
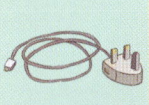 charger
 mouse
 computer
 page
 controller
 plug
 dictionary
 printer
 envelope
 screen
 friend
 socket
 internet
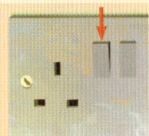 switch
 jigsaw
 tablet

Do you have any of the things in the picture at home?

Our home

bush

tent

 bat  pond

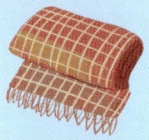 blanket  shadow

 fire  shed

 to look  space rocket

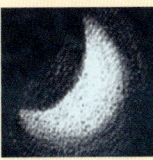 moon  star

 planet  telescope

 plant pot  wall

 to point  to yawn

 light  dark

What other things can you find in a garden?

Our home

blind

	class		playground
	to count		pupil
	desk		to read
	hook		rubber
	noticeboard		ruler
	pen		schoolbag
	pencil		scissors
	pencil case		to talk
	pencil sharpener		teacher
	to play	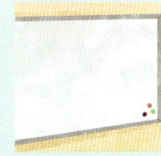	whiteboard

What have you got in your school pencil case?

At school

card

glue

 crayon
 gold
 to draw
 green
 glitter
 grey
 paint
 orange
 to paint
 pink
 tape
 purple
 colours
 red
 black
 silver
 blue
 white
 brown
 yellow

What are the children drawing and making?

At school

queue

 apple

 apron

 banana

 to carry

 chair

 to cook

 dessert

 to drink

 to eat

 fork

 hungry

 knife

 lunch

 pasta

 recycling bin

 rubbish

 sandwich

 spoon

 thirsty

 to wash up

What do you like to have for lunch?

At school

 baseball cap

 photographer

 camera

 plaster

 to catch

 to run

 cut

 to skip

 to fall

 skipping rope

 head teacher

 to take a photo

 to hop

 to throw

 to jump

 trainer

 medal

 winner

What sports day activity do you like to do?

At school

tights

 artist

 astronaut

 beard

 belt

 builder

 crown

 firefighter

 glasses

 hammer

 handbag

 helmet

 king

 necklace

 pilot

 pocket

 police officer

 queen

 ring

 scientist

 watch

Who would you like to dress up as?

At school

 audience		 light	
 band		 to listen	
 to clap		 microphone	
 to dance		 music	
 drum		 piano	
 drumsticks		 recorder	
 excited		 to sing	
 guitar		 speaker	
 instrument		 violin	

What do you think is the best instrument to play?

At school

 to kick

pitch

	ball		player
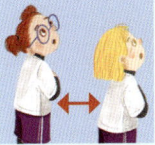	beside		ponytail
	bin		referee
	crowd		score
	flask		sweatshirt
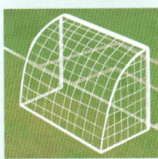	goal		team
	goalkeeper		tracksuit
	jacket		water bottle
	mug		whistle
	happy		sad

What games do you play with your friends?

At school

	to balance		roller-skate
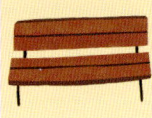	bench		roundabout
	bike		scooter
	to climb		see-saw
	to jog		skateboard
	newspaper		slide
	to push		swing
	to ride		wheel
	clean		dirty

How many children are at the park today?

Places we go

sun cream

 bucket	 spade
 cave	 to splash
 flag	 sunglasses
 island	 sunhat
 lifeguard	 surfboard
 sandal	 surfer
 sandcastle	 to swim
 shell	 swimming costume
 ship	 wave

What are the people at the beach doing?

Places we go

golf club

	badminton		shuttlecock
	basketball		strong
	bat		table tennis
	to bounce		tennis
	golf		tennis ball
	gym		tennis racket
	to hit		trampoline
	rugby		volleyball
	down		up

What sport do you like best?

Places we go

poster

reception

 bandage  ill

 cold 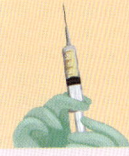 injection

 to cough  phone

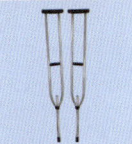 crutches  stomach ache

 dentist 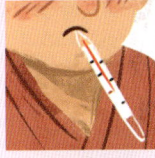 temperature

 doctor  toothache

 earache  wheelchair

 headache  to write

 to help 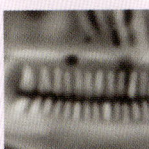 X-ray

 to sit  to stand

How many patients can you see?

Places we go 55

waiter

can

menu

 candle  pepper

 chicken  prawn

 chopsticks  rice

 fish  salad

 fries  salt

 meal  sauce

 napkin  to smell

 noodles  soup

 oil  sushi

 peas  to taste

What do you like to eat for dinner

Places we go

cloud

 baby

 panda

 bear

 penguin

 buggy

 polar bear

 child

 prizes

 to drop

 seal

 helicopter

 snack van

 ice cream

 tired

 koala

 whale

 man

 woman

 asleep

 awake

Which prize do you like best?

Places we go

	balloon		girl
	biscuit		milkshake
	bottle		present
	boy		to smile
	game		sweets
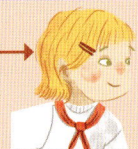	blonde		dark
	to cry		to laugh
	open		closed
	short		long
	straight		curly

What do you like to do at parties?

Places we go

On a picnic

Track 35

cricket

hill

river

 ant

 hot-air balloon

 backpack

 juice

 cake

 mango

 chocolate

 orange

 crisps

 pie

 dummy

 rope

 to fish

 to sleep

 fly

 strawberry

 food

 tomato

 grapes

 watermelon

Which food in the picnic do you like and which food don't you like?

Places we go

 arrow		 suitcase	
 to clean		 taxi	
 cleaner		 ticket	
 driver		 ticket office	
 passenger		 track	
 person		 train	
 sign		 to wave	
 to get on		 to get off	
 to lose		 to find	

How often do you travel by train or by metro?

Out and about

 apartment
 hotel
 balcony
 museum
 bank
 pedestrian crossing
 building
 supermarket
 bus
 theatre
 cinema
 traffic lights
 to cross
 tram
 to drive
 umbrella
 garage
 to wait

What is your favourite place in the city centre?

Out and about

 airport
 lorry
 ambulance
 mechanic
 car park
 motorbike
 charging point
 petrol station
 coach
 plane
 cone
 smoke
 factory
 traffic
 to fix
 tyre
 hospital
 van

How many different vehicles can you name?

Out and about

 bag
 money
 bookshop
 purse
 to buy
 shoe
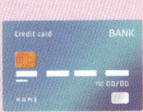 card
 shoe shop
 clothes shop
 shop assistant
 entrance
 shorts
 exit
 skirt
 to go shopping
 till
 hairband
 toy shop
 jumper
 wallet

What does your favourite shop sell?

Out and about

	bakery		library
	bus stop		meat
	butcher	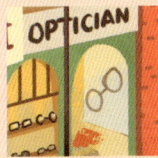	optician
	café		police car
	chemist		police station
	fire engine		post office
	fire station		statue
	hairdresser		tower
	loud		quiet

What can you buy in the town?

Out and about 73

chilli

 avocado  green beans

 basket  jug

 carrot  lemon

 cheese  nut

 coconut  onion

 cucumber  pear

 customer  pepper

 fruit  pineapple

 garlic  sweetcorn

 ginger  vegetables

What's your favourite vegetable?

Out and about

 bee

 fur

 chick

 goat

 chicken

 hay

 to dig

 horse

 donkey

 mouse

 duck

 stable

 farmer

 tractor

 to feed

 vet

 fat

 thin

What noises do the animals on the farm make?

Out and about

camel

 beak  palm tree

 beetle  parrot

 cactus  rock

 emu  sand dune

 to fly  scorpion

 hump  snake

 kangaroo  stone

Which of these animals or plants do you have where you live?

The world around us

snowboard

	air		scarf
	boot		selfie
	castle		to skate
	eagle		to ski
	forest		ski lift
	glove		skis
	hat		sledge
	ice-skate		snowball
	mountain		snowman
	to roll		tunnel

What would you like to do in the mountains?

The world around us

hedge

 bird  nest

 camper van  rabbit

 cow  rainbow

 field  sheep

 hedgehog  stream

 hole  tail

 horse-riding  to walk

 kite  welly

 magnifying glass  wood

 map  worm

How many different animals can you see?

The world around us

dolphin

 boat

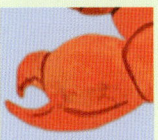 claw

 coral

 crab

 to dive

 diver

 fin

 fish

 jellyfish

 lobster

 mask

 octopus

 seaweed

 shark

 shell

 starfish

 striped

 turtle

What is your favourite thing underwater?

The world around us

 animals
 lion
 to chase
 ostrich
 feather
 ranger
 flamingo
 rhino
 to hide
 tree
 hippo
 volcano
 horn
 zebra

giraffe

Which of these animals or birds do you like best?

The world around us

In the rainforest

waterfall

 butterfly
 monkey
 canoe
 paw
 crocodile
 snail
 elephant
 spider
 frog
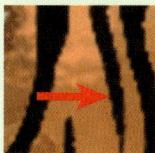 stripe
 leaf
 to swing
 leopard
 web

Which animals do you think are dangerous?

The world around us

Index

Aa

above	prep	14
afternoon	n	12
a hundred	num	17
air	n	80–81
airport	n	68–69
alphabet	n	34–35
ambulance	n	68–69
animal	n	86–87
ankle	n	19
ant	n	62–63
apartment	n	66–67
apple	n	38–39
April	n	11
apron	n	38–39
arm	n	19
armchair	n	26–27
arrow	n	64–65
art	n	18
artist	n	42–43
asleep	adj	58–59
astronaut	n	42–43
audience	n	44–45
August	n	11
aunt	n	8–9
autumn	n	13
avocado	n	74–75
awake	adj	58–59

Bb

baby	n	58–59
back	n	19
backpack	n	62–63
badminton	n	52–53
bag	n	70–71
bakery	n	72–73
[to] balance	v	48–49
balcony	n	66–67
ball	n	46–47
balloon	n	60–61
banana	n	38–39
band	n	44–45
bandage	n	54–55
bank	n	66–67
barn	n	76–77
baseball cap	n	40–41
basket	n	74–75
basketball	n	52–53
bat (animal)	n	32–33
bat (sport)	n	52–53
bath	n	24–25
bathmat	n	24–25
bathroom	n	24–25
battery	n	30–31
beach	n	50–51
beak	n	78–79
bear	n	58–59
beard	n	42–43
bed	n	22–23
bedroom	n	22–23
bee	n	76–77
beetle	n	78–79
behind	prep	14
below	prep	14
belt	n	42–43
bench	n	48–49
[to] be online	v	30–31
beside	prep	46–47
between	prep	14
big	adj	60–61
bike	n	48–49
bin	n	46–47
bird	n	82–83
biscuit	n	60–61
black	n	36–37
blanket	n	32–33
blind	n	34–35
blonde	adj	60–61
blue	n	36–37
board game	n	26–27
boat	n	84–85
body	n	19
bone	n	86–87
book	n	26–27
bookcase	n	26–27
bookshop	n	70–71
boot	n	80–81
bottle	n	60–61
[to] bounce	v	52–53
bow	n	44–45
bowl	n	28–29
boy	n	60–61
branch	n	82–83
bread	n	28–29
breakfast	n	28–29
bridge	n	64–65
broken	adj	58–59
brother	n	8–9
brown	n	36–37
brush	n	38–39
[to] brush	v	24–25
bubble	n	84–85
bucket	n	50–51
buggy	n	58–59
builder	n	42–43
building	n	66–67
bus	n	66–67
bush	n	32–33
bus stop	n	72–73
butcher	n	72–73
butterfly	n	88–89
[to] buy	v	70–71

Cc

cactus	n	78–79
café	n	72–73
cafeteria	n	38–39
cake	n	62–63
calculator	n	30–31
calendar	n	11
camel	n	78–79
camera	n	40–41
camper van	n	82–83
camping	n	82–83
can	n	56–57
candle	n	56–57
canoe	n	88–89
car	n	20–21
card (to give)	n	36–37
card (for bank)	n	70–71
car park	n	68–69
carpet	n	26–27
carrot	n	74–75
[to] carry	v	38–39
castle	n	80–81
cat	n	76–77
[to] catch	v	40–41
cave	n	50–51
cereal	n	28–29
chair	n	38–39
[to] charge	v	30–31
charger	n	30–31
charging point	n	68–69
[to] chase	v	86–87
cheese	n	74–75
chemist	n	72–73
chest of drawers	n	22–23
chick	n	76–77
chicken (food)	n	56–57
chicken (animal)	n	76–77

child *n*	58–59
chilli *n*	74–75
chocolate *n*	62–63
chopstick *n*	56–57
cinema *n*	66–67
circle *n*	19
city *n*	66–67
[to] clap *v*	44–45
class *n*	34–35
classroom *n*	34–35
claw *n*	84–85
clean *adj*	48–49
[to] clean *v*	64–65
cleaner *n*	64–65
cliff *n*	50–51
[to] climb *v*	48–49
climbing frame *n*	48–49
clock *n*	26–27
closed *adj*	60–61
clothes *pl n*	70–71
clothes shop *n*	70–71
cloud *n*	58–59
cloudy *adj*	12
coach *n*	68–69
coat *n*	80–81
coconut *n*	74–75
coffee *n*	28–29
cold *adj*	12
cold *n*	54–55
colour *n*	36–37
comb *n*	24–25
comic *n*	26–27
computer *n*	30–31
computing *n*	18
cone *n*	68–69
controller *n*	30–31
cook *n*	38–39
[to] cook *v*	38–39
cooker *n*	28–29
coral *n*	84–85
costume *n*	44–45
[to] cough *v*	54–55
[to] count *v*	34–35
countryside *n*	82–83
cousin *n*	8–9
cow *n*	82–83
crab *n*	84–85
crayon *n*	36–37
cricket *n*	62–63
crisp *n*	62–63
crocodile *n*	88–89
[to] cross *v*	66–67

crowd *n*	46–47
crown *n*	42–43
crutch *n*	54–55
[to] cry *v*	60–61
cub *n*	86–87
cucumber *n*	74–75
cup *n*	28–29
cupboard *n*	24–25
curly *adj*	60–61
curtain *n*	22–23
cushion *n*	26–27
customer *n*	74–75
cut *n*	40–41
[to] cut *v*	36–37

Dd

dad *n*	8–9
[to] dance *v*	44–45
dancer *n*	44–45
dark (at night) *adj*	32–33
dark (hair) *adj*	60–61
daughter *n*	8–9
day (of week) *n*	10
day (daylight) *n*	12
December *n*	11
delivery driver *n*	20–21
dentist *n*	54–55
desert *n*	78–79
desk *n*	34–35
dessert *n*	38–39
dictionary *n*	30–31
[to] dig *v*	76–77
dinner *n*	56–57
dinosaur *n*	26–27
direction *n*	15
dirty *adj*	48–49
dishwasher *n*	28–29
[to] dive *v*	84–85
diver *n*	84–85
doctor *n*	54–55
dog *n*	76–77
doll *n*	22–23
dolphin *n*	84–85
donkey *n*	76–77
door *n*	20–21
doorbell *n*	20–21
doormat *n*	20–21
down *adv*	52–53
downstairs *adv*	20–21
[to] draw *v*	36–37
dress *n*	22–23
dressing gown *n*	42–43

[to] dress up *v*	22–23
[to] drink *v*	38–39
[to] drive *v*	66–67
driver *n*	64–65
[to] drop *v*	58–59
drum *n*	44–45
drumstick *n*	44–45
dry *adj*	24–25
duck *n*	76–77
dummy *n*	62–63
duvet *n*	22–23

Ee

eagle *n*	80–81
ear *n*	19
earache *n*	54–55
east *n*	15
[to] eat *v*	38–39
egg *n*	28–29
eight *num*	16
eighteen *num*	17
eighty *num*	17
elbow *n*	19
elephant *n*	88–89
eleven *num*	17
emu *n*	78–79
English *n*	18
entrance *n*	70–71
envelope *n*	30–31
escalator *n*	70–71
evening *n*	12
excited *adj*	44–45
exit *n*	70–71
eye *n*	19

Ff

face *n*	19
face cloth *n*	24–25
factory *n*	68–69
falcon *n*	78–79
[to] fall *v*	40–41
family *n*	8–9
farm *n*	76–77
farmer *n*	76–77
fat *adj*	76–77
father *n*	8–9
feather *n*	86–87
February *n*	11
[to] feed *v*	76–77
fence *n*	20–21
field *n*	82–83
fifteen *num*	17

fifty *num*		17
film *n*		26–27
fin *n*		84–85
[to] find *v*		64–65
finger *n*		19
fire *n*		32–33
fire engine *n*		72–73
firefighter *n*		42–43
fire station *n*		72–73
first *adj*		40–41
fish (food) *n*		56–57
fish (animal) *n*		84–85
[to] fish *v*		62–63
five *num*		16
[to] fix *v*		68–69
flag *n*		50–51
flamingo *n*		86–87
flask *n*		46–47
floor *n*		38–39
flower *n*		26–27
fly *n*		62–63
[to] fly *v*		78–79
foggy *adj*		12
food *n*		62–63
foot *n*		19
football *n*		46–47
forest *n*		80–81
fork *n*		38–39
forty *num*		17
fountain *n*		72–73
four *num*		16
fourteen *num*		17
Friday *n*		10
fridge *n*		28–29
friend *n*		30–31
fries *pl n*		56–57
frog *n*		88–89
fruit *n*		74–75
frying pan *n*		28–29
funfair *n*		58–59
fur *n*		76–77

Gg

game *n*		60–61
games console *n*		30–31
garage *n*		66–67
garden *n*		32–33
garlic *n*		74–75
gate *n*		20–21
geography *n*		18
[to] get dressed *v*		22–23
[to] get off *v*		64–65

[to] get on *v*		64–65
[to] get up *v*		22–23
ginger *n*		74–75
giraffe *n*		86–87
girl *n*		60–61
glass *n*		28–29
glasses *pl n*		42–43
glitter *n*		36–37
glove *n*		80–81
glue *n*		36–37
goal *n*		46–47
goalkeeper *n*		46–47
goat *n*		76–77
gold *n*		36–37
golf *n*		52–53
golf club *n*		52–53
[to] go shopping *v*		70–71
grandad *n*		8–9
grandfather *n*		8–9
grandma *n*		8–9
grandmother *n*		8–9
grandparent *n*		8–9
grape *n*		62–63
grass *n*		32–33
grasslands *pl n*		86–87
green *n*		36–37
green bean *n*		74–75
grey *n*		36–37
guitar *n*		44–45
gym *n*		52–53

Hh

hair *n*		19
hairband *n*		70–71
hairbrush *n*		22–23
hairdresser *n*		72–73
half past *phr*		13
hall *n*		26–27
hammer *n*		42–43
hand *n*		19
handbag *n*		42–43
happy *adj*		46–47
hat *n*		80–81
hay *n*		76–77
head *n*		19
headache *n*		54–55
headphones *pl n*		30–31
head teacher *n*		40–41
health centre *n*		54–55
hedge *n*		82–83
hedgehog *n*		82–83
helicopter *n*		58–59

helmet *n*		42–43
[to] help *v*		54–55
[to] hide *v*		86–87
hill *n*		62–63
hippo *n*		86–87
history *n*		18
[to] hit *v*		52–53
hole *n*		82–83
homework *n*		28–29
honey *n*		28–29
hook *n*		34–35
[to] hop *v*		40–41
horn *n*		86–87
horse *n*		76–77
horse-riding *n*		82–83
hospital *n*		68–69
hot *adj*		12
hot-air balloon *n*		62–63
hotel *n*		66–67
hour *n*		13
house *n*		20–21
hump *n*		78–79
hundred *num*		17
hungry *adj*		38–39
husband *n*		8–9

Ii

ice *n*		80–81
ice cream *n*		58–59
ice-skate *n*		80–81
icy *adj*		12
ill *adj*		54–55
in *prep*		14
in front of *phr*		14
injection *n*		54–55
instrument *n*		44–45
internet *n*		30–31
island *n*		50–51

Jj

jacket *n*		46–47
jam *n*		28–29
January *n*		11
jeans *pl n*		22–23
jellyfish *n*		84–85
jigsaw *n*		30–31
[to] jog *v*		48–49
judo *n*		52–53
jug *n*		74–75
juice *n*		62–63
July *n*		11
[to] jump *v*		40–41

jumper *n*		70–71
June *n*		11

Kk

kangaroo *n*		78–79
kettle *n*		28–29
key *n*		20–21
keyboard (for music) *n*		22–23
keyboard (for computer) *n*		30–31
[to] kick *v*		46–47
king *n*		42–43
kitchen *n*		28–29
kite *n*		82–83
kitten *n*		76–77
knee *n*		19
knife *n*		38–39
koala *n*		58–59

Ll

ladder *n*		32–33
lake *n*		80–81
lamp *n*		26–27
laptop *n*		30–31
[to] laugh *v*		60–61
leaf *n*		88–89
left *adv*		15
leg *n*		19
lemon *n*		74–75
leopard *n*		88–89
lesson *n*		36–37
letter (to send) *n*		20–21
letter (in alphabet) *n*		34–35
letter box *n*		20–21
library *n*		72–73
lifeguard *n*		50–51
lift *n*		70–71
light *adj*		32–33
light *n*		44–45
line *n*		46–47
lion *n*		86–87
[to] listen *v*		44–45
little *adj*		60–61
living room *n*		26–27
lizard *n*		88–89
lobster *n*		84–85
log *n*		32–33
long *adj*		60–61
[to] look *v*		32–33
lorry *n*		68–69
[to] lose *v*		64–65
loud *adj*		72–73
lunch		38–39
lunch box *n*		38–39

Mm

magazine *n*		26–27
magnifying glass *n*		82–83
man *n*		58–59
mango *n*		62–63
map *n*		82–83
March *n*		11
market *n*		74–75
mask *n*		84–85
maths *n*		18
May *n*		11
me *pron*		8–9
meal *n*		56–57
meat *n*		72–73
mechanic *n*		68–69
medal *n*		40–41
medicine *n*		24–25
menu *n*		56–57
message *n*		72–73
metro *n*		64–65
microphone *n*		44–45
microwave *n*		28–29
midday *n*		13
midnight *n*		13
milk *n*		28–29
milkshake *n*		60–61
minute *n*		13
mirror *n*		24–25
mobile phone *n*		26–27
model *n*		36–37
Monday *n*		10
money *n*		70–71
monkey *n*		88–89
month *n*		11
moon *n*		32–33
mop *n*		64–65
morning *n*		12
mother *n*		8–9
motorbike *n*		68–69
motorway *n*		68–69
mountain *n*		80–81
mouse (for computer) *n*		30–31
mouse (animal) *n*		76–77
mouth *n*		19
mug *n*		46–47
mum *n*		8–9
museum *n*		66–67
mushroom *n*		82–83
music *n*		44–45

Nn

napkin *n*		56–57
neck *n*		19
necklace *n*		42–43
neighbour *n*		20–21
nest *n*		82–83
net *n*		52–53
newspaper *n*		48–49
night *n*		12
nine *num*		16
nineteen *num*		17
ninety *num*		17
noodle *n*		56–57
north *n*		15
nose *n*		19
noticeboard *n*		34–35
November *n*		11
number *n*		16-17
nurse *n*		54–55
nut *n*		74–75

Oo

oasis *n*		78–79
ocean *n*		84–85
o'clock *adv*		13
October *n*		11
octopus *n*		84–85
office *n*		30–31
oil *n*		56–57
olive *n*		74–75
on *prep*		14
one *num*		16
onion *n*		74–75
open *adj*		60–61
opposite *prep*		14
optician *n*		72–73
orange (colour) *n*		36–37
orange (fruit) *n*		62–63
ostrich *n*		86–87
oval *n*		19
oven *n*		28–29

Pp

page *n*		30–31
paint *n*		36–37
[to] paint *v*		36–37
paintbrush *n*		36–37
palm tree *n*		78–79
panda *n*		58–59

paper *n*		36–37
parent *n*		8–9
park *n*		48–49
parking space *n*		68–69
parrot *n*		78–79
party *n*		60–61
passenger *n*		64–65
pasta *n*		38–39
path *n*		48–49
patient *n*		54–55
pavement *n*		66–67
paw *n*		88–89
PE *n*		18
pea *n*		56–57
pear *n*		74–75
pedestrian crossing *n*		66–67
pen *n*		34–35
pencil *n*		34–35
pencil case *n*		34–35
pencil sharpener *n*		34–35
penguin *n*		58–59
pepper (spice) *n*		56–57
pepper (vegetable) *n*		74–75
person *n*		64–65
petrol station *n*		68–69
phone *n*		54–55
photo *n*		26–27
photographer *n*		40–41
piano *n*		44–45
picnic *n*		62–63
picture *n*		26–27
pie *n*		62–63
pillow *n*		22–23
pilot *n*		42–43
pineapple *n*		74–75
pink *n*		36–37
pitch *n*		46–47
pizza *n*		60–61
plane *n*		68–69
planet *n*		32–33
plant *n*		26–27
plant pot *n*		32–33
plaster *n*		40–41
plastic *n*		38–39
plate *n*		56–57
platform *n*		64–65
[to] play *v*		34–35
player *n*		46–47
playground *n*		34–35
plug *n*		30–31
pocket *n*		42–43
[to] point *v*		32–33
polar bear *n*		58–59
police car *n*		72–73
police officer *n*		42–43
police station *n*		72–73
pond *n*		32–33
ponytail *n*		46–47
postal worker *n*		20–21
postbox *n*		20–21
poster *n*		54–55
post office *n*		72–73
popcorn *n*		26–27
pot *n*		28–29
potato *n*		74–75
prawn *n*		56–57
present *n*		60–61
printer *n*		30–31
prize *n*		58–59
puddle *n*		48–49
[to] pull *v*		80–81
pupil *n*		34–35
puppy *n*		76–77
purple *n*		36–37
purse *n*		70–71
[to] push *v*		48–49
pyjamas *pl n*		22–23

Qq

quarter past *phr*		13
quarter to *phr*		13
queen *n*		42–43
queue *n*		38–39
quiet *adj*		72–73

Rr

rabbit *n*		82–83
race *n*		40–41
radio *n*		28–29
rainbow *n*		82–83
rainforest *n*		88–89
raining *v*		12
ranger *n*		86–87
[to] read *v*		34–35
reception *n*		54–55
recorder *n*		44–45
rectangle *n*		19
recycling bin *n*		38–39
red *n*		36–37
referee *n*		46–47
remote control *n*		26–27
restaurant *n*		56–57
rhino *n*		86–87
rice *n*		56–57
ride *n*		48–49
[to] ride *v*		58–59
right *adv*		15
ring *n*		42–43
river *n*		62–63
road *n*		66–67
robot *n*		22–23
rock *n*		78–79
[to] roll *v*		80–81
rollercoaster *n*		58–59
roller-skate *n*		48–49
roof *n*		20–21
rope *n*		62–63
roundabout *n*		48–49
rubber *n*		34–35
rubbish *n*		38–39
rug *n*		22–23
rugby *n*		52–53
ruler *n*		34–35
[to] run *v*		40–41

Ss

sad *adj*		46–47
salad *n*		56–57
salt *n*		56–57
sand *n*		50–51
sandal *n*		50–51
sandcastle *n*		50–51
sand dune *n*		78–79
sandpit *n*		48–49
sandwich *n*		38–39
Saturday *n*		10
sauce *n*		56–57
scales *pl n*		24–25
scarf *n*		80–81
school *n*		44–45
schoolbag *n*		34–35
science *n*		18
scientist *n*		42–43
scissors *pl n*		34–35
scooter *n*		48–49
score *n*		46–47
scorpion *n*		78–79
screen *n*		30–31
sea *n*		50–51
seal *n*		58–59
season *n*		13
seaweed *n*		84–85
second *adj*		40–41
see-saw *n*		48–49
selfie *n*		80–81

September *n*	11	
seven *num*	16	
seventeen *num*	17	
seventy *num*	17	
shadow *n*	32–33	
shampoo *n*	24–25	
shape *n*	19	
shark *n*	84–85	
shed *n*	32–33	
sheep *n*	82–83	
shelf *n*	24–25	
shell (on beach) *n*	50–51	
shell (on animal) *n*	84–85	
ship *n*	50–51	
shirt *n*	22–23	
shoe *n*	70–71	
shoe shop *n*	70–71	
shop *n*	64–65	
shop assistant *n*	70–71	
shopping centre *n*	70–71	
short (small) *adj*	60–61	
short (hair) *adj*	60–61	
shorts *pl n*	70–71	
shoulder *n*	19	
show *n*	44–45	
shower *n*	24–25	
shuttlecock *n*	52–53	
sign *n*	64–65	
silver *n*	36–37	
[to] sing *v*	44–45	
singer *n*	44–45	
sink *n*	24–25	
sister *n*	8–9	
[to] sit *v*	54–55	
six *num*	16	
sixteen *num*	17	
sixty *num*	17	
[to] skate *v*	80–81	
skateboard *n*	48–49	
ski *n*	80–81	
[to] ski *v*	80–81	
ski lift *n*	80–81	
[to] skip *v*	40–41	
skipping rope *n*	40–41	
skirt *n*	70–71	
sky *n*	82–83	
sledge *n*	80–81	
[to] sleep *v*	62–63	
slide *n*	48–49	
slipper *n*	22–23	
[to] smell *v*	56–57	
[to] smile *v*	60–61	
smoke *n*	68–69	
snack van *n*	58–59	
snail *n*	88–89	
snake *n*	78–79	
snow *n*	80–81	
snowball *n*	80–81	
snowboard *n*	80–81	
snowing *v*	12	
snowman *n*	80–81	
soap *n*	24–25	
sock *n*	22–23	
socket *n*	30–31	
sofa *n*	26–27	
son *n*	8–9	
soup *n*	56–57	
south *n*	15	
space rocket *n*	32–33	
spade *n*	50–51	
speaker *n*	44–45	
spider *n*	88–89	
[to] splash *v*	50–51	
spoon *n*	38–39	
sport *n*	40–41	
sports centre *n*	52–53	
spot *n*	22–23	
spring *n*	13	
square *n*	19	
stable *n*	76–77	
stage *n*	44–45	
stair *n*	26–27	
stall *n*	74–75	
[to] stand *v*	54–55	
star (shape) *n*	19	
star (in sky) *n*	32–33	
starfish *n*	84–85	
statue *n*	72–73	
stick *n*	82–83	
stomach *n*	19	
stomach ache *n*	54–55	
stone *n*	78–79	
stormy *adj*	12	
story *n*	34–35	
straight *adj*	60–61	
straight on *phr*	15	
strawberry *n*	62–63	
stream *n*	82–83	
street *n*	20–21	
streetlight *n*	20–21	
stripe *n*	88–89	
striped *adj*	84–85	
strong *adj*	52–53	
subject *n*	18	
sugar *n*	28–29	
suitcase *n*	64–65	
summer *n*	13	
sun *n*	86–87	
sun cream *n*	50–51	
Sunday *n*	10	
sunglasses *pl n*	50–51	
sunhat *n*	50–51	
sunny *adj*	12	
supermarket *n*	66–67	
surfboard *n*	50–51	
surfer *n*	50–51	
sushi *n*	56–57	
sweatshirt *n*	46–47	
sweet *n*	60–61	
sweetcorn *n*	74–75	
[to] swim *v*	50–51	
swimming costume *n*	50–51	
swimming pool *n*	52–53	
swing *n*	48–49	
[to] swing *v*	88–89	
switch *n*	30–31	

Tt

table *n*	26–27
tablecloth *n*	56–57
tablet *n*	30–31
table tennis *n*	52–53
tail *n*	82–83
[to] take a photo *v*	40–41
[to] talk *v*	34–35
tall *adj*	60–61
tap *n*	24–25
tape *n*	36–37
[to] taste *v*	56–57
taxi *n*	64–65
tea *n*	28–29
teacher *n*	34–35
team *n*	46–47
teddy *n*	22–23
teeth *pl n*	19
telescope *n*	32–33
television *n*	26–27
temperature *n*	54–55
ten *num*	16
tennis *n*	52–53
tennis ball *n*	52–53
tennis racket *n*	52–53
tent *n*	32–33
theatre *n*	66–67
thin *adj*	76–77

third *adj*		40–41
thirsty *adj*		38–39
thirteen *num*		17
thirty *num*		17
three *num*		16
[to] throw *v*		40–41
Thursday *n*		10
ticket *n*		64–65
ticket office *n*		64–65
tie *n*		42–43
tiger *n*		88–89
tights *pl n*		42–43
till *n*		70–71
time *n*		13
tired *adj*		58–59
toast *n*		28–29
toe *n*		19
toilet *n*		24–25
toilet paper *n*		24–25
tomato *n*		62–63
toothache *n*		54–55
toothbrush *n*		24–25
toothpaste *n*		24–25
torch *n*		32–33
towel *n*		24–25
tower *n*		72–73
town *n*		72–73
toy *n*		22–23
toy box *n*		22–23
toy shop *n*		70–71
track *n*		64–65
tracksuit *n*		46–47
tractor *n*		76–77
traffic *n*		68–69
traffic lights *pl n*		66–67
train *n*		64–65
trainer *n*		40–41
train station *n*		64–65
tram *n*		66–67
trampoline *n*		52–53
tray *n*		38–39
tree *n*		86–87
triangle *n*		19
trousers *pl n*		22–23
trunk *n*		88–89
T-shirt *n*		22–23
Tuesday *n*		10
tunnel *n*		80–81
turtle *n*		84–85
tusk *n*		88–89
twelve *num*		17
twenty *num*		17
two *num*		16
tyre *n*		68–69

Uu

umbrella *n*	66–67
uncle *n*	8–9
under *prep*	14
underwater *adj*	84–85
uniform *n*	42–43
up *adv*	52–53
upstairs *adv*	20–21

Vv

van *n*	68–69
vase *n*	26–27
vegetable *n*	74–75
vet *n*	76–77
video game *n*	30–31
village *n*	80–81
violin *n*	44–45
volcano *n*	86–87
volleyball *n*	52–53

Ww

[to] wait *v*	66–67
waiter *n*	56–57
waiting room *n*	54–55
waitress *n*	56–57
[to] walk *v*	82–83
wall *n*	32–33
wallet *n*	70–71
wardrobe *n*	22–23
[to] wash *v*	24–25
washing machine *n*	38–39
[to] wash up *v*	28–29
watch *n*	26–27
[to] watch *v*	42–43
water *n*	24–25
water bottle *n*	46–47
waterfall *n*	88–89
watermelon *n*	62–63
wave *n*	50–51
[to] wave *v*	64–65
weather *n*	12
web *n*	88–89
Wednesday *n*	10
week *n*	10
weekend *n*	10
welly *n*	82–83
west *n*	15

wet *adj*	24–25
whale *n*	58–59
wheel *n*	48–49
wheelchair *n*	54–55
whistle *n*	46–47
white *n*	36–37
whiteboard *n*	34–35
wife *n*	8–9
window *n*	20–21
windy *adj*	12
wing *n*	78–79
winner *n*	40–41
winter *n*	13
woman *n*	58–59
wood *n*	82–83
worm *n*	82–83
[to] write *v*	54–55

Xx

X-ray *n*	54–55

Yy

[to] yawn *v*	32–33
year *n*	11
yellow *n*	36–37

Zz

zebra *n*	86–87
zero *num*	16–17